THE DECLARATION OF INDEPENDENCE

AND

THE CONSTITUTION OF THE UNITED STATES

THE DECLARATION OF INDEPENDENCE

AND

THE CONSTITUTION OF THE UNITED STATES

With an introduction
by Jon Meacham

THE MODERN LIBRARY

NEW YORK

The Modern Library
An imprint of Random House
A division of Penguin Random House LLC
1745 Broadway, New York, NY 10019
modernlibrary.com
randomhousebooks.com
penguinrandomhouse.com

2025 Modern Library Edition
Introduction copyright © 2025 by Merewether LLC

Transcriptions of the Declaration of Independence, the Constitution, and
Constitutional Amendments are reproduced from the official records of the
U.S. National Archives and Records Administration.

Hardcover ISBN 979-8-217-15452-4
Ebook ISBN 979-8-217-15453-1

Printed in Canada on acid-free paper

4 6 8 9 7 5 3

BOOK TEAM: Production editor and copy editor: Michelle Daniel •
Managing editor: Rebecca Berlant • Production manager: Sandra Sjursen •
Proofreaders: Jill Falzoi, Muriel Jorgensen, and Christopher Ross

The authorized representative in the EU for product safety and compliance is
Penguin Random House Ireland, Morrison Chambers, 32 Nassau Street, Dublin
D02 YH68, Ireland. https://eu-contact.penguin.ie

CONTENTS

INTRODUCTION

By Jon Meacham

Everything seemed to be coming apart. It was the winter of 1860–61, and the American South was greeting the November election of Abraham Lincoln with secession, imperiling the Union. Watching from his home in Springfield, Illinois, Lincoln returned in his mind to the first principles of the nation he was now charged with saving. He was, interestingly, in correspondence with Alexander Stephens of Georgia, with whom he had served in Congress in the 1840s and who would soon become the vice president of the Confederacy. "You think slavery is *right* and ought to be extended; while we think it is *wrong* and ought to be restricted," Lincoln wrote Stephens on Saturday, December 22, 1860. "That I suppose is the rub."

Stephens was representative of a white South that felt surrounded, powerless, *judged*. The North, he believed, had become rabid about slavery. "When men come under the influence of fanaticism, there is no telling where their impulses or passions may drive them," Stephens replied to Lincoln. "This is what creates our discontent and apprehensions.... A word fitly spoken by you now would be like 'apples of gold in pictures of silver.'" The phrase was from the book of Proverbs, and Stephens wanted reassurance (a "word fitly spoken") that Lincoln would allow slavery to endure and even grow.

Lincoln considered the verse in a different light. In a set of private notes, the president-elect wrote that America's "apple of gold"—its most valuable asset—was the Declaration of Independence, the charter drafted, approved, and promulgated in the summer of 1776. The country's "picture of silver"—the essential frame in which the apple of gold could rest—was the Constitution, the governing document written in 1787, ratified in 1788, and put fully into operation in 1789. "Without the *Constitution* and the *Union,* we could not have attained" our national greatness, Lincoln wrote; "but even these are not the primary cause of our great prosperity. There is something back of these, entwining itself more closely about the human heart. That something, is the principle of 'Liberty to all'—the principle that clears the *path* for all—gives *hope* to all—and, by consequence, *enterprise,* and *industry* to all." As Lincoln saw it, he could not retreat from the conviction that slavery was ultimately incompatible with the spirit of the Declaration of Independence. "As I would not be a *slave,* so I would not be a *master,*" Lincoln remarked. "This expresses my idea of democracy."

Such thoughts were vital in Lincoln's cataclysmic hour, and they are vital today. If America is to be America, the foundational documents reprinted here must be not theoretical but tactile, not quaint but vivid, not dead but alive. For all our faults, for all our dreams deferred and our unfulfilled promises, the United States of America is founded not on ethnicity but on an ideal. This is not a sentimental patriotic point; it is a statement of fact. History tells us that we can chart our national progress in terms of how close we come to, or how far we fall from, realizing the implications of the Declaration and accordingly interpreting or amending our Constitution—and ourselves.

Lincoln went to Washington determined to preserve the apple of gold within its picture of silver. Through storm and strife and blood and fire he rescued the American project. To understand that project, and why he fought for its survival, we must begin at the beginning.

—

On Friday, June 7, 1776, Richard Henry Lee of Virginia rose in the Second Continental Congress to propose a resolution "that these united colonies are and of right ought to be free and independent states." Lee's motion had been a long time coming. The end of the Seven Years' War in 1763 had left Britain in a powerful position in North America, but empires are expensive things. About ten thousand British troops were deployed to defend British North America against French and Native American forces. To London, asking the colonists to bear a measure of the burden was eminently reasonable, a view that led to clashes over taxation, control of Western lands, and sea traffic. "The Americans have made a discovery, or think they have made one, that we mean to oppress them," the Anglo-Irish statesman Edmund Burke remarked in 1769. "We have made a discovery, or think we have made one, that they intend to rise in rebellion.... We know not how to advance; they know not how to retreat." In April 1775, blood was shed at Lexington and Concord. In August, King George III issued a "Proclamation for Suppressing Rebellion and Sedition," asserting that the Americans were in "open and avowed rebellion."

In November the royal governor of Virginia, Lord Dunmore, offered liberty to any enslaved person who took up arms against the rebels. Then came devastating May 1776 news that the king had hired mercenaries to help subdue his subjects.

It was in this charged climate that Richard Henry Lee offered his resolution. The Congress authorized a small committee to draft a declaration—Benjamin Franklin of Pennsylvania, John Adams of Massachusetts, Roger Sherman of Connecticut, Robert Livingston of New York, and Thomas Jefferson of Virginia. The main drafting fell to Jefferson; he undertook it, he recalled, to make the thinking of "the American mind" clear to a watching world. Writing in his redbrick boardinghouse at Seventh and Market streets in Philadelphia, Jefferson drew on Locke, Montesquieu, and the philosophers of the Scottish Enlightenment. James Wilson's pamphlet *Considerations on the Nature and Extent of the Legislative Authority of the British Parliament* and the Virginia Declaration of Rights, written by George Mason, were also influential.

In retrospect the Declaration would take on eternal significance. In real time, however, Jefferson, writing quickly in a crowded hour, saw the Declaration in practical terms. The task, he recalled, was "to place before mankind the common sense of the subject" in "terms so plain and firm as to command ... assent, and to justify ourselves in the independent stand we [felt] compelled to take.... All its authority rests then on the harmonizing sentiments of the day, whether expressed in conversation, in letters, printed essays or in the elementary books of public right, as Aristotle, Cicero, Locke, Sidney Etc." By the end of his life,

Jefferson would come to see the Declaration as something akin to scripture. He had written his draft on a mahogany lap desk of his own design that he gave to the husband of a granddaughter in 1825, observing: "Politics as well as Religion has its superstitions. These, gaining strength with time, may, one day, give imaginary value to this relic, for its great association with the birth of the Great Charter of our Independence." The ordinary had become sacred.

The document was ratified on Thursday, July 4, 1776, and the news of independence was announced on the following Monday, July 8, in front of the Pennsylvania State House. In the streets, a crowd cheered: "God bless the free states of North America."

To encounter the Declaration of Independence is to be plunged back into a complex political world. By the 1770s, the English Civil War, the Restoration, and the Glorious Revolution had shaped the American view of power. In Britain in the seventeenth century, the people, including many aristocrats, had rebelled against the absolutism of the Stuart kings, leading to chaos. There was the execution of Charles I, the commonwealth under Oliver Cromwell, the Restoration of the Stuarts (which led to more political and religious strife), and finally the Glorious Revolution of 1688–89, when William of Orange and his wife, Mary, were crowned to preside over a constitutional ethos based on a Declaration of Rights that limited the monarchy's power. The Parliament, "full and free," would be supreme, with guaranteed elections and limitations on the state's power to encroach on individual rights.

Which was essentially what the American colonists wanted: the full benefits of Englishmen, including representation in Parliament. And the denial of these rights drove much of the Declaration, which included twenty-seven grievances. These sections made up the largest portion of a document intended to convince particular audiences—wavering colonists, soldiers, potential foreign allies—of the rightness of the American cause. Congress ordered that the Declaration be distributed "to the several assemblies, conventions and committees, or councils of safety, and to the several commanding officers of the continental troops; that it be proclaimed in each of the United States, and at the head of the army."

One part of Jefferson's draft did not survive the collective (and, to the sensitive Jefferson, anguishing) editing of the Congress: a denunciation of slavery. "The clause... reprobating the enslaving [of] the inhabitants of Africa, was struck out in complaisance to South Carolina & Georgia who had never attempted to restrain the importation of slaves, and who on the contrary still wished to continue it," Jefferson noted. "Our Northern brethren also I believe felt a little tender under those censures; for tho' their people have very few slaves themselves yet they had been pretty considerable carriers of them to others."

The durability of slavery in a revolution devoted to human equality lies at the heart of the great tragedy of American history. In the world in which the Declaration was written, race-based human enslavement was seen by many white Americans as a "necessary evil," a legacy of the British Empire that could only be eradicated over time. Later, in the nineteenth century, when abolition became a more significant political force, proponents of slavery would shift their ground to argue that the institution was "a positive good"—something to be defended rather than merely endured. The resolution of these tensions would not come until the Civil War and the Thirteenth, Fourteenth, and Fifteenth Amendments to the Constitution.

An animating spirit of that struggle was Lincoln's conviction that the Declaration's assertion of innate equality was the nation's North Star. "All honor to Jefferson," Lincoln wrote in 1859, "the man who, in the concrete pressure of a struggle for national independence by a single people, had the coolness, forecast, and capacity to introduce into a merely revolutionary document, an abstract truth, applicable to all men and all times, and so to embalm it there, that to-day, and in all coming days, it shall be a rebuke and a stumbling-block to the very harbingers of re-appearing tyranny and oppression."

Applicable to all men and all times: With this claim, Lincoln elevated the Declaration to primacy of place in the American canon, work he continued at Gettysburg, Pennsylvania, in the fall of 1863. "Four score and seven years ago," he said there, "our fathers brought forth on this continent, a new nation, conceived in Liberty, and dedicated to the proposition that all men are created equal." A century later, on the steps of the memorial a grateful nation had erected to Lincoln, Martin Luther King, Jr., would tell the world about his dream—one in which America would "rise up and live out the true meaning of its creed: We hold these truths to be self-evident, that all men are created equal."

The words were Jefferson's, the aspirations universal, and the urgency as tangible as it was in that distant Philadelphia summer. "God preserve the United States," John

Page of Virginia had written Jefferson after the Declaration was adopted. "We know the race is not to the swift nor the battle to the strong. Do you not think an angel rides in the whirlwind and directs this storm?"

———

Whirlwind and storm were fitting images to evoke the politics of the years between the Declaration and the Constitution. Governed by an ineffectual Confederation Congress, the nation was largely incapable of managing its domestic or foreign affairs. Without a strong central government, the former British colonies could be vulnerable to domestic chaos and to foreign powers seeking influence in the New World. Free of London's dominion after the Treaty of Paris ended the Revolutionary War in 1783, the United States was a fragile enterprise, with authority concentrated in governors and state legislatures who saw other states not as brethren but as rivals. "Our affairs," wrote John Jay of New York, "seem to lead to some crisis... something that I cannot foresee, or conjecture."

On Monday, September 25, 1786, in western Massachusetts, events came to a head. Armed and angry farmers led by a Revolutionary veteran, Daniel Shays, rebelled after the state legislature levied a burdensome tax. Already heavily indebted and unable to win relief from property foreclosures, about 1,500 rebels captured the courthouse in Springfield. "We learn that great commotions are prevailing in Massachusetts," the diminutive and scholarly statesman James Madison wrote. "An appeal to the sword is exceedingly dreaded."

Armed rebellion terrified much of the American elite. In Boston, Samuel Adams took the warring farmers to task.

"Rebellion against a king may be pardoned," he wrote, "but the man who dares to rebel against the laws of a republic ought to suffer death." George Washington was open about his own fears in a letter written on Sunday, November 5: "We are fast verging to anarchy & confusion!"

The answer was a convention, to be held in Philadelphia. It was a heady time; the company alone was dazzling. Madison and Washington came from Virginia; Alexander Hamilton and Gouverneur Morris, who would write the immortal Preamble to the Constitution, arrived from New York. "America has certainly, upon this occasion, drawn forth her first characters," George Mason remarked. Cheering crowds heralded Washington's march into Philadelphia on Sunday, May 13, 1787. The general headquartered himself at Robert Morris's mansion on Sixth and Market and immediately called on Dr. Franklin. A few evenings later Franklin gave a large dinner party, as the host himself recalled, for "what the French call *une assemblée des notables.*"

From Friday, May 25, to Monday, September 17, 1787, fifty-five delegates met in convention to draft a constitution. It was the longest of summers. As a rule, the convention broke up at four o'clock most afternoons even, James Wilson of Pennsylvania recalled, "if a member was in the middle of his speech." (Or, one can't help thinking, *because* a member was in the middle of his speech.) The delegates veered from the most specific of questions (ratios of representation, for example, or compensation for lawmakers) to the most universal of themes about American destiny.

A guiding philosophical precept was an appreciation of human weakness and folly. Imbued with a Calvinist view of the world in which humankind was considered sinful and prone to self-interest, the framers divided power to check passions and balance competing forces. In a twenty-first-century hour of doubt and distrust about American democracy, the story of the Constitution resonates—not because the nation's founding documents came from Olympus, but because they were forged in familiar fires of war and uncertainty, of factions and fervor, of frailties and contingencies.

The essential element was the need for a government with sufficient means to guard against excesses, either by the populace or by the institutions of government. What, Madison asked, were the "ends to be served" by the new constitution? His answer: "These were first to protect the people against their rulers: secondly to protect the people against the transient impressions into which they themselves might be led."

Madison first raised the issue of slavery on the floor of the convention. "We have seen the mere distinction of colour made in the most enlightened period of time, a ground of the most oppressive dominion ever exercised by man over man," he told delegates in June. Abolitionist sentiment, however, lacked sufficient force to alter the prevailing system of race-based slavery. Nearly half (about twenty-five) of the delegates to the convention—including Madison—owned slaves, and the final document included slavery-related compromises, including the three-fifths clause, which gave slave states an advantage in the House of Representatives and in the Electoral College. Crucially, though, Madison also insisted that he "thought it wrong to admit in the Constitution the idea that there could be property in men . . . as slaves are not like merchandize, consumed, &c." This refusal to include slavery as an enumer-

ated right was part of a general antislavery sentiment—
a sentiment Frederick Douglass would recognize in the
next century when he wrote that "the Constitution of the
United States...is not a pro-slavery instrument." It was,
Douglass said, a "Glorious Liberty Document."

Once past the Constitution's stirring opening words—
"We the People of the United States, in Order to form a
more perfect Union"—the document makes for dry read-
ing. But there is something reassuring in that dryness,
something calming—as if in a world of tumult and shadow
there are also rules and light. The making of the Constitution is an instance of a large truth: The end of politics in a
democracy is to find a workable consensus while preserv-
ing a due measure of liberty. Little can be more complicated; little can be more important.

The complicated and important Constitution was signed
at the State House on Monday, September 17, 1787. Benjamin
Franklin remarked that he had often contemplated the
painting of a sun on the back of George Washington's chair
in the chamber. "Often and often in the course of the Session, and [in] the vicissitudes of my hopes and fears as to its
issue," Franklin said, he had "looked at that behind the
President without being able to tell whether it was rising or
setting: But now at length I have the happiness to know that
it is a rising and not a setting Sun."

With Franklin's words, the convention adjourned. "The
business being thus closed," Washington wrote in his diary,
the delegates dined at the City Tavern on Second near
Walnut, "and took a cordial leave of each other."

They could not know, but could only hope, that their
work would one day be lauded. "I have always regarded

that Constitution," the British statesman William Ewart Gladstone was to observe, "as the most remarkable work known to me in modern times to have been produced by the human intellect, at a single stroke (so to speak), in its application to political affairs." It was not perfect. But it was good. And that was something.

The Constitution, Abraham Lincoln believed, was forged to give expression to the Declaration. It was a means to an end—and the end was the recognition and the preservation of individual liberty and individual dignity, for without liberty and dignity humankind becomes not vessels of the divine but bodies to be commanded. Lincoln knew this. "The *Union,* and the *Constitution,* are the *picture* of *silver,* subsequently framed around" the apple of gold of the Declaration, Lincoln wrote to himself on the eve of his presidency. "The picture was made, not to *conceal,* or *destroy* the apple; but to *adorn,* and *preserve* it." Both must be cherished. Both must be defended. Both must endure. "So let us act," Lincoln said, "that neither *picture,* or *apple* shall ever be blurred, or bruised or broken."

———

JON MEACHAM is a Pulitzer Prize–winning biographer and the Rogers Chair in the American Presidency at Vanderbilt University. He is the author of the *New York Times* bestsellers *And There Was Light: Abraham Lincoln and the American Struggle, His Truth Is Marching On: John Lewis and the Power of Hope, The Soul of America, The Hope of Glory: Reflections on the Last Words of Jesus, Destiny and Power: The American Odyssey of George Herbert Walker Bush, Thomas Jefferson: The Art of Power, American Lion: Andrew Jackson in the White House, American Gospel,* and *Franklin and Winston.*

THE DECLARATION OF INDEPENDENCE

IN CONGRESS, JULY 4, 1776

The unanimous Declaration
of the thirteen united States of America

WHEN in the Course of human events, it becomes necessary for one people to dissolve the political bands which have connected them with another, and to assume among the powers of the earth, the separate and equal station to which the Laws of Nature and of Nature's God entitle them, a decent respect to the opinions of mankind requires that they should declare the causes which impel them to the separation.

We hold these truths to be self-evident, that all men are created equal, that they are endowed by their Creator with certain unalienable Rights, that among these are Life, Liberty and the pursuit of Happiness.—That to secure these rights, Governments are instituted among Men, deriving their just powers from the consent of the governed,—That whenever any Form of Government becomes destructive of these ends, it is the Right of the People to alter or to abolish it, and to institute new Government, laying its foundation on such principles and organizing its powers in such form, as to them shall seem most likely to effect their Safety and Happiness. Prudence, indeed, will dictate that

Governments long established should not be changed for light and transient causes; and accordingly all experience hath shewn, that mankind are more disposed to suffer, while evils are sufferable, than to right themselves by abolishing the forms to which they are accustomed. But when a long train of abuses and usurpations, pursuing invariably the same Object evinces a design to reduce them under absolute Despotism, it is their right, it is their duty, to throw off such Government, and to provide new Guards for their future security.—Such has been the patient sufferance of these Colonies; and such is now the necessity which constrains them to alter their former Systems of Government. The history of the present King of Great Britain is a history of repeated injuries and usurpations, all having in direct object the establishment of an absolute Tyranny over these States. To prove this, let Facts be submitted to a candid world.

He has refused his Assent to Laws, the most wholesome and necessary for the public good.

He has forbidden his Governors to pass Laws of immediate and pressing importance, unless suspended in their operation till his Assent should be obtained; and when so suspended, he has utterly neglected to attend to them.

He has refused to pass other Laws for the accommodation of large districts of people, unless those people would relinquish the right of Representation in the Legislature, a right inestimable to them and formidable to tyrants only.

He has called together legislative bodies at places unusual, uncomfortable, and distant from the depository of their public Records, for the sole purpose of fatiguing them into compliance with his measures.

He has dissolved Representative Houses repeatedly, for opposing with manly firmness his invasions on the rights of the people.

He has refused for a long time, after such dissolutions, to cause others to be elected; whereby the Legislative powers, incapable of Annihilation, have returned to the People at large for their exercise; the State remaining in the mean time exposed to all the dangers of invasion from without, and convulsions within.

He has endeavoured to prevent the population of these States; for that purpose obstructing the Laws for Naturalization of Foreigners; refusing to pass others to encourage their migrations hither, and raising the conditions of new Appropriations of Lands.

He has obstructed the Administration of Justice, by refusing his Assent to Laws for establishing Judiciary powers.

He has made Judges dependent on his Will alone, for the tenure of their offices, and the amount and payment of their salaries.

He has erected a multitude of New Offices, and sent hither swarms of Officers to harrass our people, and eat out their substance.

He has kept among us, in times of peace, Standing Armies without the Consent of our legislatures.

He has affected to render the Military independent of and superior to the Civil power.

He has combined with others to subject us to a jurisdiction foreign to our constitution, and unacknowledged by our laws; giving his Assent to their Acts of pretended Legislation:

For Quartering large bodies of armed troops among us:

For protecting them, by a mock Trial, from punishment for any Murders which they should commit on the Inhabitants of these States:

For cutting off our Trade with all parts of the world:

For imposing Taxes on us without our Consent:

For depriving us in many cases, of the benefits of Trial by Jury:

For transporting us beyond Seas to be tried for pretended offences:

For abolishing the free System of English Laws in a neighbouring Province, establishing therein an Arbitrary government, and enlarging its Boundaries so as to render it at once an example and fit instrument for introducing the same absolute rule into these Colonies:

For taking away our Charters, abolishing our most valuable Laws, and altering fundamentally the Forms of our Governments:

For suspending our own Legislatures, and declaring themselves invested with power to legislate for us in all cases whatsoever.

He has abdicated Government here, by declaring us out of his Protection and waging War against us.

He has plundered our seas, ravaged our Coasts, burnt our towns, and destroyed the lives of our people.

He is at this time transporting large Armies of foreign Mercenaries to compleat the works of death, desolation and tyranny, already begun with circumstances of Cruelty & perfidy scarcely paralleled in the most barbarous ages, and totally unworthy the Head of a civilized nation.

He has constrained our fellow Citizens taken Captive on the high Seas to bear Arms against their Country, to become the executioners of their friends and Brethren, or to fall themselves by their Hands.

He has excited domestic insurrections amongst us, and has endeavoured to bring on the inhabitants of our frontiers, the merciless Indian Savages, whose known rule of warfare, is an undistinguished destruction of all ages, sexes and conditions.

In every stage of these Oppressions We have Petitioned for Redress in the most humble terms: Our repeated Petitions have been answered only by repeated injury. A Prince whose character is thus marked by every act which may define a Tyrant, is unfit to be the ruler of a free people.

Nor have We been wanting in attentions to our Brittish brethren. We have warned them from time to time of attempts by their legislature to extend an unwarrantable jurisdiction over us. We have reminded them of the circumstances of our emigration and settlement here. We have appealed to their native justice and magnanimity, and we have conjured them by the ties of our common kindred to disavow these usurpations, which, would inevitably interrupt our connections and correspondence. They too have been deaf to the voice of justice and of consanguinity. We must, therefore, acquiesce in the necessity, which denounces our Separation, and hold them, as we hold the rest of mankind, Enemies in War, in Peace Friends.

We, therefore, the Representatives of the united States of America, in General Congress, Assembled, appealing to the Supreme Judge of the world for the rectitude of our intentions, do, in the Name, and by Authority of the good People of these Colonies, solemnly publish and declare, That these United Colonies are, and of Right ought to be Free and Independent States; that they are Absolved from all Allegiance to the British Crown, and that all political connection between them and the State of Great Britain, is and ought to be totally dissolved; and that as Free and Independent States, they have full Power to levy War, conclude Peace, contract Alliances, establish Commerce, and to do all other Acts and Things which Independent States may of right do. And for the support of this Declaration, with a firm reliance on the protection of divine Providence, we mutually pledge to each other our Lives, our Fortunes and our sacred Honor.

GEORGIA

Button Gwinnett
Lyman Hall

George Walton

NORTH CAROLINA

William Hooper
Joseph Hewes

John Penn

SOUTH CAROLINA

Edward Rutledge
Thomas Heyward, Jr.

Thomas Lynch, Jr.
Arthur Middleton

MASSACHUSETTS

John Hancock

MARYLAND

Samuel Chase
William Paca
Thomas Stone

Charles Carroll of
Carrollton

VIRGINIA

George Wythe
Richard Henry Lee
Thomas Jefferson
Benjamin Harrison
Thomas Nelson, Jr.

Francis Lightfoot Lee
Carter Braxton

PENNSYLVANIA

Robert Morris
Benjamin Rush
Benjamin Franklin
John Morton
George Clymer

James Smith
George Taylor
James Wilson
George Ross

DELAWARE

Caesar Rodney
George Read

Thomas McKean

NEW YORK

William Floyd
Philip Livingston

Francis Lewis
Lewis Morris

NEW JERSEY

Richard Stockton
John Witherspoon
Francis Hopkinson

John Hart
Abraham Clark

NEW HAMPSHIRE

Josiah Bartlett

William Whipple

MASSACHUSETTS

Samuel Adams
John Adams

Robert Treat Paine
Elbridge Gerry

RHODE ISLAND

Stephen Hopkins

William Ellery

CONNECTICUT

Roger Sherman
Samuel Huntington

William Williams
Oliver Wolcott

NEW HAMPSHIRE

Matthew Thornton

THE CONSTITUTION OF
THE UNITED STATES

WE THE PEOPLE *of the United States, in Order to form a more perfect Union, establish Justice, insure domestic Tranquility, provide for the common defence, promote the general Welfare, and secure the Blessings of Liberty to ourselves and our Posterity, do ordain and establish this Constitution for the United States of America.*

ARTICLE I

Section 1

All legislative Powers herein granted shall be vested in a Congress of the United States, which shall consist of a Senate and House of Representatives.

Section 2

The House of Representatives shall be composed of Members chosen every second Year by the People of the several States, and the Electors in each State shall have the Qualifications requisite for Electors of the most numerous Branch of the State Legislature.

No Person shall be a Representative who shall not have attained to the Age of twenty five Years, and been seven Years a Citizen of the United States, and who shall not, when elected, be an Inhabitant of that State in which he shall be chosen.

Representatives and direct Taxes shall be apportioned among the several States which may be included within this Union, according to their respective Numbers, which shall be determined by adding to the whole Number of free Persons, including those bound to Service for a Term of Years, and excluding Indians not taxed, three fifths of all other Persons.* The actual Enumeration shall be made within three Years after the first Meeting of the Congress of the United States, and within every subsequent Term of ten Years, in such Manner as they shall by Law direct. The Number of Representatives shall not exceed one for every thirty Thousand, but each State shall have at Least one Representative; and until such enumeration shall be made, the State of New Hampshire shall be entitled to chuse three, Massachusetts eight, Rhode-Island and Providence Plantations one, Connecticut five, New-York six, New Jersey four, Pennsylvania eight, Delaware one, Maryland six, Virginia ten, North Carolina five, South Carolina five, and Georgia three.

When vacancies happen in the Representation from any State, the Executive Authority thereof shall issue Writs of Election to fill such Vacancies.

The House of Representatives shall chuse their Speaker and other Officers; and shall have the sole Power of Impeachment.

Section 3

The Senate of the United States shall be composed of two Senators from each State, chosen by the Legislature

---

* Modified by section 2 of the 14th amendment.

thereof, for six Years; and each Senator shall have one Vote.

Immediately after they shall be assembled in Consequence of the first Election, they shall be divided as equally as may be into three Classes. The Seats of the Senators of the first Class shall be vacated at the Expiration of the second Year, of the second Class at the Expiration of the fourth Year, and of the third Class at the Expiration of the sixth Year, so that one third may be chosen every second Year; and if Vacancies happen by Resignation, or otherwise, during the Recess of the Legislature of any State, the Executive thereof may make temporary Appointments until the next Meeting of the Legislature, which shall then fill such Vacancies.*

No Person shall be a Senator who shall not have attained to the Age of thirty Years, and been nine Years a Citizen of the United States, and who shall not, when elected, be an Inhabitant of that State for which he shall be chosen.

The Vice President of the United States shall be President of the Senate, but shall have no Vote, unless they be equally divided.

The Senate shall chuse their other Officers, and also a President pro tempore, in the Absence of the Vice President, or when he shall exercise the Office of President of the United States.

The Senate shall have the sole Power to try all Impeachments. When sitting for that Purpose, they shall be on Oath or Affirmation. When the President of the United States is

* Modified by the 17th amendment.

tried, the Chief Justice shall preside: And no Person shall be convicted without the Concurrence of two thirds of the Members present.

Judgment in Cases of Impeachment shall not extend further than to removal from Office, and disqualification to hold and enjoy any Office of honor, Trust or Profit under the United States: but the Party convicted shall nevertheless be liable and subject to Indictment, Trial, Judgment and Punishment, according to Law.

Section 4

The Times, Places and Manner of holding Elections for Senators and Representatives, shall be prescribed in each State by the Legislature thereof; but the Congress may at any time by Law make or alter such Regulations, except as to the Places of chusing Senators.

The Congress shall assemble at least once in every Year, and such Meeting shall be on the first Monday in December,* unless they shall by Law appoint a different Day.

Section 5

Each House shall be the Judge of the Elections, Returns and Qualifications of its own Members, and a Majority of each shall constitute a Quorum to do Business; but a smaller Number may adjourn from day to day, and may be authorized to compel the Attendance of absent Members, in such Manner, and under such Penalties as each House may provide.

* Modified by the 20th amendment.

Each House may determine the Rules of its Proceedings, punish its Members for disorderly Behaviour, and, with the Concurrence of two thirds, expel a Member.

Each House shall keep a Journal of its Proceedings, and from time to time publish the same, excepting such Parts as may in their Judgment require Secrecy; and the Yeas and Nays of the Members of either House on any question shall, at the Desire of one fifth of those Present, be entered on the Journal.

Neither House, during the Session of Congress, shall, without the Consent of the other, adjourn for more than three days, nor to any other Place than that in which the two Houses shall be sitting.

Section 6

The Senators and Representatives shall receive a Compensation for their Services, to be ascertained by Law, and paid out of the Treasury of the United States. They shall in all Cases, except Treason, Felony and Breach of the Peace, be privileged from Arrest during their Attendance at the Session of their respective Houses, and in going to and returning from the same; and for any Speech or Debate in either House, they shall not be questioned in any other Place.

No Senator or Representative shall, during the Time for which he was elected, be appointed to any civil Office under the Authority of the United States, which shall have been created, or the Emoluments whereof shall have been encreased during such time; and no Person holding any Office under the United States, shall be a Member of either House during his Continuance in Office.

Section 7

All Bills for raising Revenue shall originate in the House of Representatives; but the Senate may propose or concur with Amendments as on other Bills.

Every Bill which shall have passed the House of Representatives and the Senate, shall, before it become a Law, be presented to the President of the United States; If he approve he shall sign it, but if not he shall return it, with his Objections to that House in which it shall have originated, who shall enter the Objections at large on their Journal, and proceed to reconsider it. If after such Reconsideration two thirds of that House shall agree to pass the Bill, it shall be sent, together with the Objections, to the other House, by which it shall likewise be reconsidered, and if approved by two thirds of that House, it shall become a Law. But in all such Cases the Votes of both Houses shall be determined by yeas and Nays, and the Names of the Persons voting for and against the Bill shall be entered on the Journal of each House respectively. If any Bill shall not be returned by the President within ten Days (Sundays excepted) after it shall have been presented to him, the Same shall be a Law, in like Manner as if he had signed it, unless the Congress by their Adjournment prevent its Return, in which Case it shall not be a Law.

Every Order, Resolution, or Vote to which the Concurrence of the Senate and House of Representatives may be necessary (except on a question of Adjournment) shall be presented to the President of the United States; and before the Same shall take Effect, shall be approved by him, or being disapproved by him, shall be repassed by two thirds of the Senate and House of Representatives, according to the Rules and Limitations prescribed in the Case of a Bill.

Section 8

The Congress shall have Power To lay and collect Taxes, Duties, Imposts and Excises, to pay the Debts and provide for the common Defence and general Welfare of the United States; but all Duties, Imposts and Excises shall be uniform throughout the United States;

To borrow Money on the credit of the United States;

To regulate Commerce with foreign Nations, and among the several States, and with the Indian Tribes;

To establish an uniform Rule of Naturalization, and uniform Laws on the subject of Bankruptcies throughout the United States;

To coin Money, regulate the Value thereof, and of foreign Coin, and fix the Standard of Weights and Measures;

To provide for the Punishment of counterfeiting the Securities and current Coin of the United States;

To establish Post Offices and post Roads;

To promote the Progress of Science and useful Arts, by securing for limited Times to Authors and Inventors the exclusive Right to their respective Writings and Discoveries;

To constitute Tribunals inferior to the supreme Court;

To define and punish Piracies and Felonies committed on the high Seas, and Offences against the Law of Nations;

To declare War, grant Letters of Marque and Reprisal, and make Rules concerning Captures on Land and Water;

To raise and support Armies, but no Appropriation of Money to that Use shall be for a longer Term than two Years;

To provide and maintain a Navy;

To make Rules for the Government and Regulation of the land and naval Forces;

To provide for calling forth the Militia to execute the Laws of the Union, suppress Insurrections and repel Invasions;

To provide for organizing, arming, and disciplining, the Militia, and for governing such Part of them as may be employed in the Service of the United States, reserving to the States respectively, the Appointment of the Officers, and the Authority of training the Militia according to the discipline prescribed by Congress;

To exercise exclusive Legislation in all Cases whatsoever, over such District (not exceeding ten Miles square) as may, by Cession of particular States, and the Acceptance of Congress, become the Seat of the Government of the United States, and to exercise like Authority over all Places purchased by the Consent of the Legislature of the State in which the Same shall be, for the Erection of Forts, Magazines, Arsenals, dock-Yards, and other needful Buildings;—And

To make all Laws which shall be necessary and proper for carrying into Execution the foregoing Powers, and all other Powers vested by this Constitution in the Government of the United States, or in any Department or Officer thereof.

Section 9

The Migration or Importation of such Persons as any of the States now existing shall think proper to admit, shall not be prohibited by the Congress prior to the Year one thousand eight hundred and eight, but a Tax or duty may be imposed on such Importation, not exceeding ten dollars for each Person.

The Privilege of the Writ of Habeas Corpus shall not be suspended, unless when in Cases of Rebellion or Invasion the public Safety may require it.

No Bill of Attainder or ex post facto Law shall be passed.

No Capitation, or other direct, Tax shall be laid, unless in Proportion to the Census or enumeration herein before directed to be taken.*

No Tax or Duty shall be laid on Articles exported from any State.

No Preference shall be given by any Regulation of Commerce or Revenue to the Ports of one State over those of another: nor shall Vessels bound to, or from, one State, be obliged to enter, clear, or pay Duties in another.

No Money shall be drawn from the Treasury, but in Consequence of Appropriations made by Law; and a regular Statement and Account of the Receipts and Expenditures of all public Money shall be published from time to time.

No Title of Nobility shall be granted by the United States: And no Person holding any Office of Profit or Trust under them, shall, without the Consent of the Congress, accept of any present, Emolument, Office, or Title, of any kind whatever, from any King, Prince, or foreign State.

---

* Modified by the 16th amendment.

Section 10

No State shall enter into any Treaty, Alliance, or Confederation; grant Letters of Marque and Reprisal; coin Money; emit Bills of Credit; make any Thing but gold and silver Coin a Tender in Payment of Debts; pass any Bill of Attainder, ex post facto Law, or Law impairing the Obligation of Contracts, or grant any Title of Nobility.

No State shall, without the Consent of the Congress, lay any Imposts or Duties on Imports or Exports, except what may be absolutely necessary for executing it's inspection Laws: and the net Produce of all Duties and Imposts, laid by any State on Imports or Exports, shall be for the Use of the Treasury of the United States; and all such Laws shall be subject to the Revision and Controul of the Congress.

No State shall, without the Consent of Congress, lay any Duty of Tonnage, keep Troops, or Ships of War in time of Peace, enter into any Agreement or Compact with another State, or with a foreign Power, or engage in War, unless actually invaded, or in such imminent Danger as will not admit of delay.

ARTICLE II

Section 1

The executive Power shall be vested in a President of the United States of America. He shall hold his Office during the Term of four Years, and, together with the Vice President, chosen for the same Term, be elected, as follows

Each State shall appoint, in such Manner as the Legislature thereof may direct, a Number of Electors, equal to the whole Number of Senators and Representatives to which the State may be entitled in the Congress: but no Senator or Representative, or Person holding an Office of Trust or Profit under the United States, shall be appointed an Elector.

The Electors shall meet in their respective States, and vote by Ballot for two Persons, of whom one at least shall not be an Inhabitant of the same State with themselves. And they shall make a List of all the Persons voted for, and of the Number of Votes for each; which List they shall sign and certify, and transmit sealed to the Seat of the Government of the United States, directed to the President of the Senate. The President of the Senate shall, in the Presence of the Senate and House of Representatives, open all the Certificates, and the Votes shall then be counted. The Person having the greatest Number of Votes shall be the President, if such Number be a Majority of the whole Number of Electors appointed; and if there be more than one who have such Majority, and have an equal Number of Votes, then the House of Representatives shall immediately chuse by Ballot one of them for President; and if no Person have a Majority, then from the five highest on the List the said House shall in like Manner chuse the President. But in chusing the President, the Votes shall be taken by States, the Representation from each State having one Vote; A quorum for this Purpose shall consist of a Member or

Members from two thirds of the States, and a Majority of all the States shall be necessary to a Choice. In every Case, after the Choice of the President, the Person having the greatest Number of Votes of the Electors shall be the Vice President. But if there should remain two or more who have equal Votes, the Senate shall chuse from them by Ballot the Vice President.*

The Congress may determine the Time of chusing the Electors, and the Day on which they shall give their Votes; which Day shall be the same throughout the United States.

No Person except a natural born Citizen, or a Citizen of the United States, at the time of the Adoption of this Constitution, shall be eligible to the Office of President; neither shall any Person be eligible to that Office who shall not have attained to the Age of thirty five Years, and been fourteen Years a Resident within the United States.

In Case of the Removal of the President from Office, or of his Death, Resignation, or Inability to discharge the Powers and Duties of the said Office, the Same shall devolve on the Vice President, and the Congress may by Law provide for the Case of Removal, Death, Resignation or Inability, both of the President and Vice President, declaring what Officer shall then act as President, and such Officer shall act accordingly, until the Disability be removed, or a President shall be elected.†

The President shall, at stated Times, receive for his Ser-

---

* Modified by the 12th amendment.
† Modified by the 25th amendment.

vices, a Compensation, which shall neither be encreased nor diminished during the Period for which he shall have been elected, and he shall not receive within that Period any other Emolument from the United States, or any of them.

Before he enter on the Execution of his Office, he shall take the following Oath or Affirmation:—"I do solemnly swear (or affirm) that I will faithfully execute the Office of President of the United States, and will to the best of my Ability, preserve, protect and defend the Constitution of the United States."

Section 2

The President shall be Commander in Chief of the Army and Navy of the United States, and of the Militia of the several States, when called into the actual Service of the United States; he may require the Opinion, in writing, of the principal Officer in each of the executive Departments, upon any Subject relating to the Duties of their respective Offices, and he shall have Power to grant Reprieves and Pardons for Offences against the United States, except in Cases of Impeachment.

He shall have Power, by and with the Advice and Consent of the Senate, to make Treaties, provided two thirds of the Senators present concur; and he shall nominate, and by and with the Advice and Consent of the Senate, shall appoint Ambassadors, other public Ministers and Consuls, Judges of the supreme Court, and all other Officers of the United States, whose Appointments are not herein otherwise provided for, and which shall be established by Law: but the Congress may by Law vest the Appointment of such inferior Officers, as they think proper, in the President alone, in the Courts of Law, or in the Heads of Departments.

The President shall have Power to fill up all Vacancies that may happen during the Recess of the Senate, by granting Commissions which shall expire at the End of their next Session.

Section 3

He shall from time to time give to the Congress Information of the State of the Union, and recommend to their Consideration such Measures as he shall judge necessary and expedient; he may, on extraordinary Occasions, convene both Houses, or either of them, and in Case of Disagreement between them, with Respect to the Time of Adjournment, he may adjourn them to such Time as he shall think proper; he shall receive Ambassadors and other public Ministers; he shall take Care that the Laws be faithfully executed, and shall Commission all the Officers of the United States.

Section 4

The President, Vice President and all civil Officers of the United States, shall be removed from Office on Impeachment for, and Conviction of, Treason, Bribery, or other high Crimes and Misdemeanors.

ARTICLE III

Section 1

The judicial Power of the United States, shall be vested in one supreme Court, and in such inferior Courts as the Congress may from time to time ordain and establish. The Judges, both of the supreme and inferior Courts, shall hold their Offices during good Behaviour, and shall, at stated Times, receive for their Services, a Compensation, which shall not be diminished during their Continuance in Office.

Section 2

The judicial Power shall extend to all Cases, in Law and Equity, arising under this Constitution, the Laws of the United States, and Treaties made, or which shall be made, under their Authority;—to all Cases affecting Ambassadors, other public Ministers and Consuls;—to all Cases of admiralty and maritime Jurisdiction;—to Controversies to which the United States shall be a Party;—to Controversies between two or more States;—between a State and Citizens of another State,*—between Citizens of different States,—between Citizens of the same State claiming Lands under Grants of different States, and between a State, or the Citizens thereof, and foreign States, Citizens or Subjects.

* Modified by the 11th amendment.

In all Cases affecting Ambassadors, other public Ministers and Consuls, and those in which a State shall be Party, the supreme Court shall have original Jurisdiction. In all the other Cases before mentioned, the supreme Court shall have appellate Jurisdiction, both as to Law and Fact, with such Exceptions, and under such Regulations as the Congress shall make.

The Trial of all Crimes, except in Cases of Impeachment, shall be by Jury; and such Trial shall be held in the State where the said Crimes shall have been committed; but when not committed within any State, the Trial shall be at such Place or Places as the Congress may by Law have directed.

Section 3

Treason against the United States, shall consist only in levying War against them, or in adhering to their Enemies, giving them Aid and Comfort. No Person shall be convicted of Treason unless on the Testimony of two Witnesses to the same overt Act, or on Confession in open Court.

The Congress shall have Power to declare the Punishment of Treason, but no Attainder of Treason shall work Corruption of Blood, or Forfeiture except during the Life of the Person attainted.

ARTICLE IV

Section 1

Full Faith and Credit shall be given in each State to the public Acts, Records, and judicial Proceedings of every other State. And the Congress may by general Laws prescribe the Manner in which such Acts, Records and Proceedings shall be proved, and the Effect thereof.

Section 2

The Citizens of each State shall be entitled to all Privileges and Immunities of Citizens in the several States.

A Person charged in any State with Treason, Felony, or other Crime, who shall flee from Justice, and be found in another State, shall on Demand of the executive Authority of the State from which he fled, be delivered up, to be removed to the State having Jurisdiction of the Crime.

No Person held to Service or Labour in one State, under the Laws thereof, escaping into another, shall, in Consequence of any Law or Regulation therein, be discharged from such Service or Labour, but shall be delivered up on Claim of the Party to whom such Service or Labour may be due.*

---

*   Modified by the 13th amendment.

Section 3

New States may be admitted by the Congress into this Union; but no new State shall be formed or erected within the Jurisdiction of any other State; nor any State be formed by the Junction of two or more States, or Parts of States, without the Consent of the Legislatures of the States concerned as well as of the Congress.

The Congress shall have Power to dispose of and make all needful Rules and Regulations respecting the Territory or other Property belonging to the United States; and nothing in this Constitution shall be so construed as to Prejudice any Claims of the United States, or of any particular State.

Section 4

The United States shall guarantee to every State in this Union a Republican Form of Government, and shall protect each of them against Invasion; and on Application of the Legislature, or of the Executive (when the Legislature cannot be convened) against domestic Violence.

ARTICLE V

The Congress, whenever two thirds of both Houses shall deem it necessary, shall propose Amendments to this Constitution, or, on the Application of the Legislatures of two thirds of the several States, shall call a Convention for proposing Amendments, which, in either Case, shall be valid to all Intents and Purposes, as Part of this Constitution, when ratified by the Legislatures of three fourths of the several States, or by Conventions in three fourths thereof, as the one or the other Mode of Ratification may be proposed by the Congress; Provided that no Amendment which may be made prior to the Year One thousand eight hundred and eight shall in any Manner affect the first and fourth Clauses in the Ninth Section of the first Article; and that no State, without its Consent, shall be deprived of its equal Suffrage in the Senate.

ARTICLE VI

All Debts contracted and Engagements entered into, before the Adoption of this Constitution, shall be as valid against the United States under this Constitution, as under the Confederation.

This Constitution, and the Laws of the United States which shall be made in Pursuance thereof; and all Treaties made, or which shall be made, under the Authority of the United States, shall be the supreme Law of the Land; and the Judges in every State shall be bound thereby, any Thing in the Constitution or Laws of any State to the Contrary notwithstanding.

The Senators and Representatives before mentioned, and the Members of the several State Legislatures, and all executive and judicial Officers, both of the United States and of the several States, shall be bound by Oath or Affirmation, to support this Constitution; but no religious Test shall ever be required as a Qualification to any Office or public Trust under the United States.

ARTICLE VII

The Ratification of the Conventions of nine States, shall be sufficient for the Establishment of this Constitution between the States so ratifying the Same.

The Word, "the," being interlined between the seventh and eighth Lines of the first Page, The Word "Thirty" being partly written on an Erazure in the fifteenth Line of the first Page, The Words "is tried" being interlined between the thirty second and thirty third Lines of the first Page and the Word "the" being interlined between the forty third and forty fourth Lines of the second Page.

Attest William Jackson Secretary

done in Convention by the Unanimous Consent of the States present the Seventeenth Day of September in the Year of our Lord one thousand seven hundred and Eighty seven and of the Independance of the United States of America the Twelfth In witness whereof We have hereunto subscribed our Names,

G°. Washington
Presidt and deputy from Virginia

DELAWARE

Geo: Read   Richard Bassett
Gunning Bedford jun   Jaco: Broom
John Dickinson

MARYLAND

James McHenry   Danl. Carroll
Dan of St Thos. Jenifer

VIRGINIA

John Blair   James Madison Jr.

NORTH CAROLINA

Wm. Blount   Hu Williamson
Richd. Dobbs Spaight

SOUTH CAROLINA

J. Rutledge   Charles Pinckney
Charles Cotesworth   Pierce Butler
Pinckney

GEORGIA

William Few   Abr Baldwin

NEW HAMPSHIRE

John Langdon   Nicholas Gilman

MASSACHUSETTS

Nathaniel Gorham   Rufus King

CONNECTICUT

Wm. Saml. Johnson   *Roger Sherman*

NEW YORK

Alexander Hamilton

NEW JERSEY

Wil: Livingston   *Wm. Paterson*
David Brearley   *Jona: Dayton*

PENNSYLVANIA

B Franklin   *Thos. FitzSimons*
Thomas Mifflin   *Jared Ingersoll*
Robt. Morris   *James Wilson*
Geo. Clymer   *Gouv Morris*

Amendments to the Constitution: The Bill of Rights (1—10)

Amendment I

Congress shall make no law respecting an establishment of religion, or prohibiting the free exercise thereof; or abridging the freedom of speech, or of the press; or the right of the people peaceably to assemble, and to petition the Government for a redress of grievances.

Amendment II

A well regulated Militia, being necessary to the security of a free State, the right of the people to keep and bear Arms, shall not be infringed.

Amendment III

No Soldier shall, in time of peace be quartered in any house, without the consent of the Owner, nor in time of war, but in a manner to be prescribed by law.

AMENDMENT IV

The right of the people to be secure in their persons, houses, papers, and effects, against unreasonable searches and seizures, shall not be violated, and no Warrants shall issue, but upon probable cause, supported by Oath or affirmation, and particularly describing the place to be searched, and the persons or things to be seized.

AMENDMENT V

No person shall be held to answer for a capital, or otherwise infamous crime, unless on a presentment or indictment of a Grand Jury, except in cases arising in the land or naval forces, or in the Militia, when in actual service in time of War or public danger; nor shall any person be subject for the same offence to be twice put in jeopardy of life or limb; nor shall be compelled in any criminal case to be a witness against himself, nor be deprived of life, liberty, or property, without due process of law; nor shall private property be taken for public use, without just compensation.

AMENDMENT VI

In all criminal prosecutions, the accused shall enjoy the right to a speedy and public trial, by an impartial jury of the State and district wherein the crime shall have been committed, which district shall have been previously ascertained by law, and to be informed of the nature and cause of the accusation; to be confronted with the witnesses against him; to have compulsory process for obtaining witnesses in his favor, and to have the Assistance of Counsel for his defence.

AMENDMENT VII

In Suits at common law, where the value in controversy shall exceed twenty dollars, the right of trial by jury shall be preserved, and no fact tried by a jury, shall be otherwise re-examined in any Court of the United States, than according to the rules of the common law.

AMENDMENT VIII

Excessive bail shall not be required, nor excessive fines imposed, nor cruel and unusual punishments inflicted.

AMENDMENT IX

The enumeration in the Constitution, of certain rights, shall not be construed to deny or disparage others retained by the people.

AMENDMENT X

The powers not delegated to the United States by the Constitution, nor prohibited by it to the States, are reserved to the States respectively, or to the people.

AMENDMENTS TO THE
CONSTITUTION: 11—27

AMENDMENT XI

PASSED BY CONGRESS MARCH 4, 1794.
RATIFIED FEBRUARY 7, 1795.
ARTICLE III, SECTION 2, OF THE CONSTITUTION WAS MODIFIED
BY AMENDMENT 11.

The Judicial power of the United States shall not be construed to extend to any suit in law or equity, commenced or prosecuted against one of the United States by Citizens of another State, or by Citizens or Subjects of any Foreign State.

AMENDMENT XII

PASSED BY CONGRESS DECEMBER 9, 1803.
RATIFIED JUNE 15, 1804.
A PORTION OF ARTICLE II, SECTION 1 OF THE CONSTITUTION
WAS SUPERSEDED BY THE 12TH AMENDMENT.

The Electors shall meet in their respective states and vote by ballot for President and Vice-President, one of whom, at least, shall not be an inhabitant of the same state with themselves; they shall name in their ballots the person voted for as President, and in distinct ballots the person voted for as Vice-President, and they shall make distinct lists of all persons voted for as President, and of all persons voted for as Vice-President, and of the number of votes for each, which lists they shall sign and certify, and transmit sealed to the seat of the government of the United States, directed to the President of the Senate;—the President of the Senate shall, in the presence of the Senate and House of Representatives, open all the certificates and the votes shall then be counted;— The person having the greatest number of votes for President, shall be the President, if such number be a majority of the whole number of Electors appointed; and if no person have such majority, then from the persons having the highest numbers not exceeding three on the list of those voted for as President, the House of Representatives shall choose immediately, by ballot, the President. But in choosing the President, the votes shall be taken by states, the representation from each state having one vote; a quorum for this purpose shall consist of a member or members from two-thirds of the states, and a majority of all the states shall be necessary to a choice. And if the House of Representatives shall not choose a President whenever the right of choice shall devolve upon them, before the fourth day of March next following, then the Vice-President shall act as President, as in case of the death or other constitutional disability of the President.—*

The person having the greatest number of votes as Vice-

* Superseded by section 3 of the 20th amendment.

President, shall be the Vice-President, if such number be a majority of the whole number of Electors appointed, and if no person have a majority, then from the two highest numbers on the list, the Senate shall choose the Vice-President; a quorum for the purpose shall consist of two-thirds of the whole number of Senators, and a majority of the whole number shall be necessary to a choice. But no person constitutionally ineligible to the office of President shall be eligible to that of Vice-President of the United States.

AMENDMENT XIII

PASSED BY CONGRESS JANUARY 31, 1865.
RATIFIED DECEMBER 6, 1865.
A PORTION OF ARTICLE IV, SECTION 2, OF THE CONSTITUTION
WAS SUPERSEDED BY THE 13TH AMENDMENT.

Section 1

Neither slavery nor involuntary servitude, except as a punishment for crime whereof the party shall have been duly convicted, shall exist within the United States, or any place subject to their jurisdiction.

Section 2

Congress shall have power to enforce this article by appropriate legislation.

AMENDMENT XIV

PASSED BY CONGRESS JUNE 13, 1866. RATIFIED JULY 9, 1868.
ARTICLE I, SECTION 2, OF THE CONSTITUTION WAS MODIFIED
BY SECTION 2 OF THE 14TH AMENDMENT.

Section 1

All persons born or naturalized in the United States, and subject to the jurisdiction thereof, are citizens of the United States and of the State wherein they reside. No State shall make or enforce any law which shall abridge the privileges or immunities of citizens of the United States; nor shall any State deprive any person of life, liberty, or property, without due process of law; nor deny to any person within its jurisdiction the equal protection of the laws.

Section 2

Representatives shall be apportioned among the several States according to their respective numbers, counting the whole number of persons in each State, excluding Indians not taxed. But when the right to vote at any election for the choice of electors for President and Vice-President of the United States, Representatives in Congress, the Executive and Judicial officers of a State, or the members of the Legislature thereof, is denied to any of the male inhabitants of such State, being twenty-one years of age,* and citizens of

---

* Changed by section 1 of the 26th amendment.

the United States, or in any way abridged, except for participation in rebellion, or other crime, the basis of representation therein shall be reduced in the proportion which the number of such male citizens shall bear to the whole number of male citizens twenty-one years of age in such State.

Section 3

No person shall be a Senator or Representative in Congress, or elector of President and Vice-President, or hold any office, civil or military, under the United States, or under any State, who, having previously taken an oath, as a member of Congress, or as an officer of the United States, or as a member of any State legislature, or as an executive or judicial officer of any State, to support the Constitution of the United States, shall have engaged in insurrection or rebellion against the same, or given aid or comfort to the enemies thereof. But Congress may by a vote of two-thirds of each House, remove such disability.

Section 4

The validity of the public debt of the United States, authorized by law, including debts incurred for payment of pensions and bounties for services in suppressing insurrection or rebellion, shall not be questioned. But neither the United States nor any State shall assume or pay any debt or obligation incurred in aid of insurrection or rebellion against the United States, or any claim for the loss or emancipation of any slave; but all such debts, obligations and claims shall be held illegal and void.

Section 5

The Congress shall have power to enforce, by appropriate legislation, the provisions of this article.

AMENDMENT XV

PASSED BY CONGRESS FEBRUARY 26, 1869.
RATIFIED FEBRUARY 3, 1870.

Section 1

The right of citizens of the United States to vote shall not be denied or abridged by the United States or by any State on account of race, color, or previous condition of servitude—

Section 2

The Congress shall have power to enforce this article by appropriate legislation.

AMENDMENT XVI

PASSED BY CONGRESS JULY 2, 1909. RATIFIED FEBRUARY 3, 1913.
ARTICLE I, SECTION 9, OF THE CONSTITUTION WAS MODIFIED
BY AMENDMENT 16.

The Congress shall have power to lay and collect taxes on incomes, from whatever source derived, without apportionment among the several States, and without regard to any census or enumeration.

AMENDMENT XVII

PASSED BY CONGRESS MAY 13, 1912. RATIFIED APRIL 8, 1913.
ARTICLE I, SECTION 3, OF THE CONSTITUTION WAS MODIFIED
BY THE 17TH AMENDMENT.

The Senate of the United States shall be composed of two Senators from each State, elected by the people thereof, for six years; and each Senator shall have one vote. The electors in each State shall have the qualifications requisite for electors of the most numerous branch of the State legislatures.

When vacancies happen in the representation of any State in the Senate, the executive authority of such State shall issue writs of election to fill such vacancies: Provided, That the legislature of any State may empower the executive thereof to make temporary appointments until the people fill the vacancies by election as the legislature may direct.

This amendment shall not be so construed as to affect the election or term of any Senator chosen before it becomes valid as part of the Constitution.

AMENDMENT XVIII

PASSED BY CONGRESS DECEMBER 18, 1917.
RATIFIED JANUARY 16, 1919. REPEALED BY AMENDMENT 21.

Section 1

After one year from the ratification of this article the manufacture, sale, or transportation of intoxicating liquors within, the importation thereof into, or the exportation thereof from the United States and all territory subject to the jurisdiction thereof for beverage purposes is hereby prohibited.

Section 2

The Congress and the several States shall have concurrent power to enforce this article by appropriate legislation.

Section 3

This article shall be inoperative unless it shall have been ratified as an amendment to the Constitution by the legislatures of the several States, as provided in the Constitution, within seven years from the date of the submission hereof to the States by the Congress.

AMENDMENT XIX

PASSED BY CONGRESS JUNE 4, 1919. RATIFIED AUGUST 18, 1920.

The right of citizens of the United States to vote shall not be denied or abridged by the United States or by any State on account of sex.

Congress shall have power to enforce this article by appropriate legislation.

AMENDMENT XX

PASSED BY CONGRESS MARCH 2, 1932.
RATIFIED JANUARY 23, 1933.
ARTICLE I, SECTION 4, OF THE CONSTITUTION WAS MODIFIED
BY SECTION 2 OF THIS AMENDMENT. IN ADDITION, A PORTION
OF THE 12TH AMENDMENT WAS SUPERSEDED BY SECTION 3.

Section 1

The terms of the President and the Vice President shall end at noon on the 20th day of January, and the terms of Senators and Representatives at noon on the 3d day of January, of the years in which such terms would have ended if this article had not been ratified; and the terms of their successors shall then begin.

Section 2

The Congress shall assemble at least once in every year, and such meeting shall begin at noon on the 3d day of January, unless they shall by law appoint a different day.

Section 3

If, at the time fixed for the beginning of the term of the President, the President elect shall have died, the Vice President elect shall become President. If a President shall not have been chosen before the time fixed for the beginning of his term, or if the President elect shall have failed to qualify, then the Vice President elect shall act as President until a President shall have qualified; and the Congress may by law provide for the case wherein neither a President elect nor a Vice President elect shall have qualified, declaring who shall then act as President, or the manner in which one who is to act shall be selected, and such person shall act accordingly until a President or Vice President shall have qualified.

Section 4

The Congress may by law provide for the case of the death of any of the persons from whom the House of Representatives may choose a President whenever the right of choice shall have devolved upon them, and for the case of the death of any of the persons from whom the Senate may choose a Vice President whenever the right of choice shall have devolved upon them.

Section 5

Sections 1 and 2 shall take effect on the 15th day of October following the ratification of this article.

Section 6

This article shall be inoperative unless it shall have been ratified as an amendment to the Constitution by the legislatures of three-fourths of the several States within seven years from the date of its submission.

AMENDMENT XXI

PASSED BY CONGRESS FEBRUARY 20, 1933.
RATIFIED DECEMBER 5, 1933.

Section 1

The eighteenth article of amendment to the Constitution of the United States is hereby repealed.

Section 2

The transportation or importation into any State, Territory, or possession of the United States for delivery or use therein of intoxicating liquors, in violation of the laws thereof, is hereby prohibited.

Section 3

This article shall be inoperative unless it shall have been ratified as an amendment to the Constitution by conventions in the several States, as provided in the Constitution, within seven years from the date of the submission hereof to the States by the Congress.

Amendment XXII

PASSED BY CONGRESS MARCH 21, 1947.
RATIFIED FEBRUARY 27, 1951.

Section 1

No person shall be elected to the office of the President more than twice, and no person who has held the office of President, or acted as President, for more than two years of a term to which some other person was elected President shall be elected to the office of the President more than once. But this Article shall not apply to any person holding the office of President when this Article was proposed by the Congress, and shall not prevent any person who may be holding the office of President, or acting as President, during the term within which this Article becomes operative from holding the office of President or acting as President during the remainder of such term.

Section 2

This article shall be inoperative unless it shall have been ratified as an amendment to the Constitution by the legislatures of three-fourths of the several States within seven years from the date of its submission to the States by the Congress.

AMENDMENT XXIII

PASSED BY CONGRESS JUNE 16, 1960. RATIFIED MARCH 29, 1961.

Section 1

The District constituting the seat of Government of the United States shall appoint in such manner as the Congress may direct:

A number of electors of President and Vice President equal to the whole number of Senators and Representatives in Congress to which the District would be entitled if it were a State, but in no event more than the least populous State; they shall be in addition to those appointed by the States, but they shall be considered, for the purposes of the election of President and Vice President, to be electors appointed by a State; and they shall meet in the District and perform such duties as provided by the twelfth article of amendment.

Section 2

The Congress shall have power to enforce this article by appropriate legislation.

AMENDMENT XXIV

PASSED BY CONGRESS AUGUST 27, 1962.
RATIFIED JANUARY 23, 1964.

Section 1

The right of citizens of the United States to vote in any primary or other election for President or Vice President, for electors for President or Vice President, or for Senator or Representative in Congress, shall not be denied or abridged by the United States or any State by reason of failure to pay any poll tax or other tax.

Section 2

The Congress shall have power to enforce this article by appropriate legislation.

Amendment XXV

PASSED BY CONGRESS JULY 6, 1965. RATIFIED FEBRUARY 10, 1967. ARTICLE II, SECTION 1, OF THE CONSTITUTION WAS AFFECTED BY THE 25TH AMENDMENT.

Section 1

In case of the removal of the President from office or of his death or resignation, the Vice President shall become President.

Section 2

Whenever there is a vacancy in the office of the Vice President, the President shall nominate a Vice President who shall take office upon confirmation by a majority vote of both Houses of Congress.

Section 3

Whenever the President transmits to the President pro tempore of the Senate and the Speaker of the House of Representatives his written declaration that he is unable to discharge the powers and duties of his office, and until he transmits to them a written declaration to the contrary, such powers and duties shall be discharged by the Vice President as Acting President.

Section 4

Whenever the Vice President and a majority of either the principal officers of the executive departments or of such other body as Congress may by law provide, transmit to the President pro tempore of the Senate and the Speaker of the House of Representatives their written declaration that the President is unable to discharge the powers and duties of his office, the Vice President shall immediately assume the powers and duties of the office as Acting President.

Thereafter, when the President transmits to the President pro tempore of the Senate and the Speaker of the House of Representatives his written declaration that no inability exists, he shall resume the powers and duties of his office unless the Vice President and a majority of either the principal officers of the executive department or of such other body as Congress may by law provide, transmit within four days to the President pro tempore of the Senate and the Speaker of the House of Representatives their written declaration that the President is unable to discharge the powers and duties of his office. Thereupon Congress shall decide the issue, assembling within forty-eight hours for that purpose if not in session. If the Congress, within twenty-one days after receipt of the latter written declaration, or, if Congress is not in session, within twenty-one days after Congress is required to assemble, determines by two-thirds vote of both Houses that the President is unable to discharge the powers and duties of his office, the Vice President shall continue to discharge the same as Acting President; otherwise, the President shall resume the powers and duties of his office.

AMENDMENT XXVI

PASSED BY CONGRESS MARCH 23, 1971. RATIFIED JULY 1, 1971. AMENDMENT 14, SECTION 2, OF THE CONSTITUTION WAS MODIFIED BY SECTION 1 OF THE 26TH AMENDMENT.

Section 1

The right of citizens of the United States, who are eighteen years of age or older, to vote shall not be denied or abridged by the United States or by any State on account of age.

Section 2

The Congress shall have power to enforce this article by appropriate legislation.

AMENDMENT XXVII

ORIGINALLY PROPOSED SEPT. 25, 1789. RATIFIED MAY 7, 1992.

No law, varying the compensation for the services of the Senators and Representatives, shall take effect, until an election of Representatives shall have intervened.

Notes to the Introduction

vii "You think slavery is *right*": Jon Meacham, *And There Was Light: Abraham Lincoln and the American Struggle* (New York, 2022), 207.

vii "When men come under": Ibid.

vii A word fitly spoken: Proverbs 25:11 (KJV).

viii "Without the *Constitution*": Meacham, *And There Was Light,* 207–8.

viii "As I would not be a *slave*": Ibid., xxi.

 ix a resolution "that these united colonies": "Lee Resolution (1776)," Milestone Documents, National Archives, https://www.archives.gov/milestone-documents/lee-resolution.

 ix The end of the Seven Years' War in 1763: For the background to the Revolutionary War, I drew on my *Thomas Jefferson: The Art of Power* (New York, 2012), 27–39, and the accompanying source notes on pages 535–44.

 ix "The Americans have made a discovery": "Speech on Townshend Duties, 19 April 1769," *The Writings and Speeches of Edmund Burke,* ed. Paul Langford (Oxford, 1981), 2:231.

 ix In April 1775: On the events leading to the Declaration of Independence, I have depended on Pauline Maier, *American Scripture: Making the Declaration of Independence* (New York, 1997), 7–46.

  x offered liberty to any enslaved person: On Dunmore, see, for instance, Michael A. McDonnell, *The Politics of War:*

Race, Class, and Conflict in Revolutionary Virginia (Chapel Hill, N.C., 2007); Benjamin Quarles, "Lord Dunmore as Liberator," *The William and Mary Quarterly*, 4th ser., vol. 15 (October 1958): 494–507.

x devastating May 1776 news: Maier, *American Scripture*, 38–39.

x "the American mind": "Extract from Thomas Jefferson to Henry Lee," May 8, 1825, Jefferson Quotes & Family Letters, https://tjrs.monticello.org/letter/436.

x his redbrick boardinghouse: "Declaration House," National Park Service, https://www.nps.gov/places/000/declaration-house.htm. See also Meacham, *Thomas Jefferson*, 99.

x Jefferson drew on Locke: Meacham, *Thomas Jefferson*, 104.

x "to place before mankind": Thomas Jefferson to Henry Lee, May 8, 1825, Founders Online, National Archives, https://founders.archives.gov/documents/Jefferson/98-01-02-5212.

xi a mahogany lap desk: "Declaration of Independence Desk," National Museum of American History, https://americanhistory.si.edu/collections/object/nmah_513641.

xi "Politics as well as Religion": Ibid.

xi "God bless the free states": Meacham, *Thomas Jefferson*, 106–7.

xi By the 1770s, the English Civil War: Ibid., 28–30.

xi "full and free": "Bill of Rights [1688]," National Archives (UK), https://www.legislation.gov.uk/aep/WillandMarSess2/1/2/introduction.

xii "to the several assemblies": "Second Continental Congress: July 4, 1776," American Founding, https://americanfounding.org/entries/second-continental-congress-july-4-1776/.

xii "The clause … reprobating": "Extract from Thomas Jefferson's Notes on the Proceedings in the Continental Congress," July 2, 1776, Jefferson Quotes & Family Letters, https://tjrs.monticello.org/letter/54.

xii a "necessary evil": "Southern Nationalism," Digital History, https://www.digitalhistory.uh.edu/disp_textbook .cfm?smtid=2&psid=3559.

xii "a positive good": Ibid.

xiii The resolution of these tensions: See, for instance, Eric Foner, *Reconstruction: America's Unfinished Revolution, 1863–1877* (New York, 1989).

xiii "All honor to Jefferson": Abraham Lincoln to Henry L. Pierce and others, April 6, 1859, Abraham Lincoln Online, https://www.abrahamlincolnonline.org/lincoln/speeches /pierce.htm.

xiii "Four score and seven years ago": Abraham Lincoln, "The Gettysburg Address," November 19, 1863, Abraham Lincoln Online, https://www.abrahamlincolnonline.org/lincoln /speeches/gettysburg.htm.

xiii "rise up and live out": Martin Luther King, Jr., "I Have a Dream," Address Delivered at the March on Washington for Jobs and Freedom, August 28, 1963, American Rhetoric, https://www.americanrhetoric.com/speeches /mlkihaveadream.htm.

xiii "God preserve the United States": Meacham, *Thomas Jefferson,* 108. See also Robert M. S. McDonald, "Thomas Jefferson's Changing Reputation as Author of the Declaration of Independence: The First Fifty Years," *Journal of the Early Republic* 19, no. 2 (Summer 1999): 169–95.

xiv "Our affairs," wrote John Jay: "To George Washington from John Jay, 27 June 1786," Founders Online, National Archives, https://founders.archives.gov/documents /Washington/04-04-02-0129.

xiv Armed and angry farmers: For Shays' Rebellion, see, for instance, Sean Wilentz, *The Rise of American Democracy: Jef-*

ferson to Lincoln (New York, 2005), 30–32, and William Hogeland, *The Whiskey Rebellion: George Washington, Alexander Hamilton, and the Frontier Rebels Who Challenged America's Newfound Sovereignty* (New York, 2006), 52–53.

xiv "We learn that": William T. Hutchinson et al., eds., *The Papers of James Madison* (1st ser., Chicago, 1962–77), 9:154.

xiv Armed rebellion terrified: The reports of violence were exaggerated, but their political effect was undeniable. See, for instance, Richard Beeman, *Plain, Honest Men: The Making of the American Constitution* (New York, 2009), 16–18; Carol Berkin, *A Brilliant Solution: Inventing the American Constitution* (New York, 2002), 26–28.

xv "Rebellion against a king": Berkin, *Brilliant Solution,* 28.

xv "We are fast verging": *Papers of James Madison,* 9:161. The quoted letter was George Washington to James Madison, November 5, 1786.

xv "America has certainly": Max Farrand, ed., *The Records of the Federal Convention* (New Haven, Conn., 1922), 3:32.

xv Cheering crowds heralded: Beeman, *Plain, Honest Men,* 34.

xv The general headquartered himself: Ibid., 34–35.

xv Franklin gave a large dinner: Ibid., 52–53.

xv broke up at four: Farrand, *Records,* 3:137–138.

xvi the "ends to be served": James Madison, *Notes of Debates in the Federal Convention of 1787* (Athens, Ohio, 1966), 193.

xvi "We have seen": Ibid., 77.

xvi Nearly half (about twenty-five): Steven Mintz, "Historical Context: The Constitution and Slavery," Gilder Lehrman Institute of American History, https://www.gilderlehrman.org/history-resources/teaching-resource/historical-context-constitution-and-slavery.

xvi slavery-related compromises: See, for instance, Paul Finkelman, *Slavery and the Founders: Race and Liberty in the Age of Jefferson* (Armonk, N.Y., 2001); James Oakes, *The Crooked*

Path to Abolition: Abraham Lincoln and the Antislavery Constitu-tion (New York, 2021); David Waldstreicher, *Slavery's Con-stitution: From Revolution to Ratification* (New York, 2009); Sean Wilentz, *No Property in Man: Slavery and Antislavery at the Nation's Founding* (Cambridge, Mass., 2018).

 xvi "thought it wrong": *Papers of James Madison,* 10:157.

xvii "the Constitution of the United States": Frederick Doug-lass, "The Constitution of the United States: Is It Pro-slavery or Anti-slavery?" March 26, 1860, BlackPast.org, https://www.blackpast.org/global-african-history/1860 -frederick-douglass-constitution-united-states-it-pro -slavery-or-anti-slavery/.

xvii "Glorious Liberty Document": Frederick Douglass, "What, to the Slave, Is the Fourth of July?" July 5, 1852, BlackPast.org, https://www.blackpast.org/african -american-history/speeches-african-american -history/1852-frederick-douglass-what-slave-fourth-july/.

xvii Benjamin Franklin remarked: Madison, *Notes of Debates,* 659.

xvii "The business": Clinton Rossiter, *1787: The Grand Convention* (New York, 1987), 237.

xvii at the City Tavern: Ibid., 238.

xvii "I have always": Christopher Collier and James Lincoln Collier, *Decision in Philadelphia: The Constitutional Convention of 1787* (New York, 1986), epigraph. See also "The Original-ity of the United States Constitution," *The Yale Law Jour-nal 5,* no. 6 (1896): 239–46, https://doi.org/10.2307/781281.

xviii "The *Union,* and the *Constitution*": Meacham, *And There Was Light,* 208.

ABOUT THE TYPE

The principal text of this Modern Library edition was set in a digitized version of Janson, a typeface that dates from about 1690 and was cut by Nicholas Kis (1650–1702), a Hungarian working in Amsterdam. The original matrices have survived and are held by the Stempel foundry in Germany. Hermann Zapf (1918–2015) redesigned some of the weights and sizes for Stempel, basing his revisions on the original design.